THE NOISE WAR

HANDBOOK

How to Fight Disinformation and Find Truth When Everything is Lying to You

J.J. Green

Copyright © 2025 J.J. Green

All rights reserved. No part of this book may be reproduced or transmitted in any form without written permission from the publisher.

ISBN: 979-8-218-86261-9

Cover design by [J.J. Green]

Published by Shondine House Publishing

Printed in the United States of America

ACKNOWLEDGEMENTS

First, I thank the creator of life for every breath and step that's led me to this work. My deepest gratitude to my incredible multi-dimensional mother, Daisy, educator, minister, and community leader, who somehow always has time to be "Mom." To my amazing genius wife, Gina, thanks for everything. Your brilliant mind and vast, diverse knowledge are matched only by your nurturing spirit and boundless energy. To my loving sisters Jackie and Karen, thank you for inspiring and supporting me all my life.

Special thanks to Jenny Beth Aloys, Dr. Yvonne Bolling, Eeva Eek-Pajuste, Dr. Lenora Peters Gant, Verena Greb, Janita Hamalainen, Charlotte Horn, Maret Koplus, Fritz Luders, Rev. William H. Lamar IV, Col. Karen "Jack" Magnus, Marianna Markarova, Kathleen Murphy, Pam Ortega, Piia Palm, Nikos Panagiotou, Gretchen Sorin, Giannis Triantafyllidis, Leonie Voss, Roz Whitaker-Heck, and the strong cadre of global journalists whose courage and commitment to accuracy inspire me.

To my colleagues at WTOP, thanks for motivating me. To Marat Mindiyarov, Gen. Michael Hayden, Dr. Hans-Jakob Schindler, and Natalia Belikova. You enriched this narrative and grounded it in hard reality.

Finally, thanks to the AFIO, American U., BBC, CBS, the Connecting Media Conference, DW Akademie, Hampton U., Howard U., the Journalists and Writers Foundation, the Lennart Meri Conference, the League of Women Voters of Cooperstown, Marymount U., Metropolitan AME Church, NDR, the Pentagon Press Association, Postimees, RAI, the Phoenix Society, the RIAS Berlin Kommission, the Riga Conference, RTDNA, SAG-AFTRA, Tech Camp, THISAM, Vermont Council on World Affairs, WJLA TV, WTTG TV and WRC TV for giving me a platform to speak and engage on this and other topics.

DEDICATION

In memory of my dad,

Rev. J.J. Green Sr.

"In this life you've got to know something for yourself."

TABLE OF CONTENTS

Part One: Understanding the Flood

Chapter One: What is "Flood the Zone"?

Chapter Two: Anatomy of a Flood

Chapter Three: What the Flood Does to Us

Chapter Four: The Thin Line Between Disinformation and Misinformation

Part Two: Strategic Countermeasures

Chapter Five: Narrow the Firehose

Chapter Six: Pre-bunking Instead of Debunking

Chapter Seven: Collective Defense — A NATO for Journalism

Part Three: Building Resilience:

Chapter Eight: Clarity Beats Clutter

Chapter Nine: Tech & Platforms — Turning Down the Volume

Chapter Ten: Audience Resilience & Media Literacy

Part Four: The Road Ahead

Chapter Eleven: Belarus and the Making of an Alternate Reality

Conclusion: Playing the Long Game

Resources

PREFACE

On October 15, 2025, I had a choice—surrender my credentials to work inside the Pentagon or sign a document pledging to report only information officially approved by the department.

I, along with dozens of other journalists, declined to do it, turned in my credential, and walked out. It wasn't an act of protest. It was an act of principle.

For three decades, my work has depended on trust, accuracy, and respect. Signing that memo would have thrown that trust and respect away.

I'm deeply committed to fighting disinformation. Agreeing to such a request would create doubt about my commitment to that principle. On June 5, 2025, in a speech to the Cooperstown, New York League of Women Voters, I pointed out that we were facing a tough fight and we all would have to eventually make "some difficult decisions".

On October 15, it was my turn, like so many other Americans before me and many more still to come.

For the last 21 years, I've reported from the front lines of global conflict—places where truth itself is often under fire. I've stood in the dust of Afghanistan as the Taliban advanced on Kabul, walked through bombed-out neighborhoods in Iraq, covered Ukraine's valiant and desperate fight against Russia, from near its western border with Poland. In those conflicts, I lost colleagues and friends; and visited the hospital rooms of others gravely injured along the way. I've also sat across from generals, spies, and survivors of wars and aggression from here in the U.S., across Europe, the Middle East and Africa, to East Asia. I've covered cyber warfare, disinformation campaigns, and the quiet operations that shape the world we never see on the evening news.

In all of those places, one thing rings true: the battle for territory has become inseparable from the battle for truth.

I wrote *The Noise War* because the information battle that once raged overseas has come home. What autocrats perfected abroad—flooding societies with lies, confusion, and doubt—has now been injected into America's own political bloodstream. The same techniques once used to destabilize Ukraine or silence journalists in Moscow are now being deployed against citizens scrolling their feeds from Milwaukee to Miami and across the U.S.

Every day, I watch disinformation metastasize: AI-generated deepfakes spreading faster than fact-checks, fabricated scandals drowning out real ones, and public trust collapsing under the weight of relentless manipulation. It's not just noise, it's a weapon. And it's aimed at the foundations of democracy: truth, accountability, and free expression.

This handbook is not a lament—it's a plan. It's not the first of its kind, but in 2025, it is unique because *The Noise War* merges journalistic practice with national security awareness, creating a unique hybrid between the UNESCO educator model and the NATO/StratCom operational framework. It carries a dual identity: part reference manual for professionals, part classroom-ready curriculum.

By fusing journalistic discipline with strategic insight, it's more than a guide—it's a bridge between the newsroom, the classroom, and the situation room, equipping readers to understand, anticipate, and counter the modern information war.

The Noise War is built for journalists trying to stay above the flood, policymakers searching for practical guardrails, schools and universities preparing students for the rest of their lives and citizens who refuse to surrender to cynicism. It draws on years of field reporting, intelligence analysis, and conversations with those who've fought the disinformation wars from Kyiv to Kigali, Tallinn to Washington.

My goal is to provide a simple, quick, easy-to-read reference guide to help readers, from high schoolers to post graduate students, see the patterns, name the tactics, and build resilience before the next wave hits.

There is hope. We are not powerless. But defense begins with understanding how the flood of disinformation works, and how to filter it. In an age when falsehoods can be engineered at scale and weaponized at speed, truth itself must become our strongest form of resistance.

The Noise War is my contribution to that fight. I encourage you to write in the margins, underline passages, and make notes anywhere you find and need space in this handbook. Make it your own, take it with you, use it, and become familiar with it because the disinformation genie is out of the bottle. We can't put it back in, but we can constrain it.

Introduction

Origins of the Flood

Are you so tired of the lies, political posturing, finger pointing, chaotic scenes of war, disaster, and deepfakes that you've turned off the TV and radio news; and you don't even look at the headlines on your digital device?

If so, that is exactly what the people and organizations peddling disinformation want—for you to walk away from it too exhausted to figure out what the truth is.

That means your information sources of choice have been likely been flooded with disinformation.

We are living through an information war, unlike any the world has ever seen. Truth itself is under siege. The battlefield is everywhere: on your phone, in your feed, in the very language we use to make sense of reality. Disinformation is no longer crafted in smoke-filled rooms—it's generated in seconds by artificial intelligence, amplified by algorithms, and unleashed by those who see chaos not as a threat, but as a weapon.

Authoritarian leaders have learned the oldest trick in the book and armed it with the newest technology: "flood the zone," drown the truth, exhaust the public until lies feel easier than facts. The result is a global fog—manufactured confusion that corrodes trust, divides societies, and weakens democracy from within.

That is why *The Noise War* exists.

This handbook is not a big, long book of theory. It's a short, simple manual for survival that I hope people *everywhere* will see and use.

It's an easy, clear read designed for journalists, educators, civic leaders, and every citizen who refuses to surrender truth to the algorithm. It offers the tools to see through the flood, to filter noise from knowledge, and to rebuild the shared reality that democracy depends on. That is important, because in an age where AI can fabricate a voice, a face, even a war—our defense must be clarity, courage, and collective vigilance.

The time for complacency is over. The flood is rising. *The Noise War Handbook* is how we learn to stand against it.

Part One:
Understanding the Flood

Chapter One
What is "Flood the Zone"?

Flood the zone.

Those three words that capture one of the most dangerous ideas of our time, the deliberate drowning of truth in a sea of noise, are not new. Hitler's minion, Goebbels, did it with film and rallies before and during World War II. The USSR's Stalin did it with newspapers and radio during the early stages of the Cold War. In the Philippines, Duterte did it, less than a decade ago, with trolls. Forces in Putin's Russia do it today, with algorithms.

American political operative Steve Bannon gave it the modern name — "Flood the Zone." "The real opposition is the media," he said. "And the way to deal with them is to flood the zone with sh**t."

It replaces debate with distraction, reason with rage, and journalism with a firehose of filth designed to blind us. This is not a method of persuasion—it's suffocation. It's the strategy of chaos: overwhelm the senses, bury the facts, and make people so exhausted by lies that they stop believing in anything. The U.S. ran head-on into this phenomenon in the mid-2010s.

It had a home address: 55 Savushkina Street, St. Petersburg, Russia.

Marat Mindiyarov, a young unemployed Russian teacher, told me how he stumbled upon it in late 2014 while looking for work.

He landed a writing job, at a media company, paying 45,000 rubles a month — good money and just a short walk from his home. The office looked ordinary, but the gray building that housed it is now known as the infamous Internet Research Agency (IRA). Inside, he found rows of cubicles occupied by people posting stories about Russia that were polished, patriotic — and patently false. He told me in an interview, "What I had to write was absolutely not true." His task was to glorify life under Vladimir Putin, to drown out reality with illusion. The more he read independent media, the more uneasy he became. He realized it wasn't journalism. It was propaganda — and he was part of it.

Marat, seeking to salvage his job and his dignity, tried to transfer to the "Facebook Department." There, the pay was double, but he had to take a writing test that revealed something much darker at play.

The topic of his quiz was "The possibility of Hillary Clinton winning the U.S. presidential election." By now, it was early 2015 — long before the actual campaign had begun in the U.S.

He wrote on the exam that it would be "cool" if Clinton became the first female U.S. president.

He failed the test, not because he wasn't smart enough, but because he was too honest.

Only later did he realize he had glimpsed the factory's secret mission: to target the United States.

Disillusioned and ashamed, he quit weeks later, saying, "To write untruths every day and be paid for it—it's something strange." His short stint helped expose one of the most audacious information warfare operations of the modern age. It was aimed squarely at the U.S., and we were not ready for it.

Soon, the lies he once wrote in St. Petersburg would echo in small-town America.

On the morning of Sept. 11, 2014, "We started getting phone calls in regard to a message titled 'toxic fumes, hazard warning,'" said Duval Arthur, director of the office of Homeland Security and Emergency Preparedness in St. Mary Parish, Louisiana.

He told me in my capacity as national security correspondent at WTOP radio in Washington, D.C., that citizens received a text message alert about 8 a.m. about an explosion at a manufacturing plant.

The alert read "'take shelter, check local media,'" according to Arthur; the dispatch was sent from Columbia Chemical Company and listed its website as columbiachemical.com.

Within two hours, social media users from the Gulf of Mexico to the Great Lakes were inundated with posts about the incident.

Twitter and other social media platforms were jammed with images of the explosion and a screenshot of a CNN homepage. Even a YouTube video had been posted showing someone watching a TV broadcast in which ISIS had allegedly claimed responsibility for an attack on the plant.

But not a word of it was true. It was all an elaborately staged hoax.

The organization mentioned in the alert, Columbia Chemical Company, did not exist.

There is a company in the area called Columbian Chemical, owned by Birla.

Arthur told me he called the company, and they said, "We have been informed by the community that a text message has been received by several individuals indicating a release of toxic gas from the Birla Carbon's Columbian Chemicals Plant near Centerville, Louisiana. The content, as stated by the text message, is not true. There has been no release of such toxic gas, explosion, or any other incident in our facility. We are not aware of the origin of this text message."

When I asked who was responsible, Arthur said, "I was told it was the Russians, but I have no information on that — none whatsoever."

A spokesperson for the FBI's New Orleans Field Office declined to comment on the disposition or nature of the inquiry.

Even though Arthur was uncertain about who was behind the incident, current and former U.S. intelligence sources were clear that it and other incidents like it were the work of a Russian government-funded network.

That network, I later learned, was indeed located in a nondescript office building, on a quiet street in St. Petersburg, Russia, just as Marat had said.

The Internet Research Agency's mission was simple but devastating: to manufacture false content and blast it at Americans through social media platforms like Twitter and Facebook.

Many users, believing they were debating fellow citizens on ordinary political issues, were actually engaging with Russian operatives. Some of those exchanges spilled into the streets—real protests and confrontations sparked by fabricated posts meant to inflame racial and political divisions. The goal wasn't persuasion but control through chaos: to drown truth in noise until people stopped trying to discern it.

This is the essence of a disinformation flood—power achieved not by silencing voices, but by overwhelming them.

Analysis:

"Flooding the Zone" is not propaganda in the traditional sense. It doesn't rely on persuasion, ideology, or even coherence. It's an act of saturation. By flooding public spaces with conflicting information, falsehoods, and emotional triggers, bad actors can drown out verified truth, manipulate attention, and paralyze decision-making.

Three core features define the tactic:

1. Volume: A deluge of content, much of it low-quality or contradictory, makes it nearly impossible to distinguish signal from noise.

2. Velocity: Falsehoods spread faster than corrections. By the time truth catches up, the damage is done.

3. Variation: Contradictions are intentional. One day, the virus is a hoax, the next it's a weapon. The confusion itself is the objective.

This tactic was perfected in Russia, tested globally, and now replicated by state and non-state actors. Flooding creates not belief, but doubt — and in a democracy, doubt is as destructive as lies.

Takeaways:

- Floods win through exhaustion, not persuasion.

- Filtering begins with recognition and disciplined focus.

- Awareness is defense; attention is power.

Toolkit:

- Use tools like Hamilton 2.0 Dashboard, Botometer, or Graphika to spot inauthentic amplification.

- Identify recurring flood patterns: contradictory narratives, emotional spikes, coordinated posting.

Exercises

Create and maintain a disinformation log: date, platform, claim, source, and how it evolved.

- Map which actors benefit from confusion — the key to attribution.

- Use the tools mentioned above to work through the exercise.

The False-Alarm Scan

Goal: Develop early recognition skills.

Reporter's Scenario: Pick a breaking rumor on your beat. In 10 minutes, list two reasons to hold coverage and two checks you must complete first.

Reflection: Which pressure (speed, competition, emotion) most tempted you to publish?

Mapping Motives

Goal: Identify beneficiaries of confusion.

Task: For one viral falsehood, list the actors who gain politically, financially, or ideologically if the claim spreads.

Reflection: How does motive shape the narrative's structure?

Chapter Two

Anatomy of a Flood

In the children's "pass-the-word" game, a simple sentence often gets twisted as it moves from one whisper to the next—misheard, rephrased, or "improved" until the final version barely resembles the original. It's harmless on the playground. But in the adult world, the same process drives misinformation. And when those distortions are pushed deliberately, repeated widely, or amplified with intent, a child's game becomes a weapon—disinformation, one capable of overrunning truth long before it reaches the last person in line.

That was a major concern in September 2025, U.S. Secret Service agents dismantled a clandestine telecom network of more than 300 Subscriber Identity Module (SIM) servers and more than 100,000 SIM cards clustered within 35 miles of the United Nations building in New York City. It was a system that former Secret Service Agent Donald Mihalek warned could blanket every cellphone in the country in about 12 minutes. A week later, through my reporting, I learned that an additional 200,000 networked phones seized in nearby New Jersey raised the total number of networked SIMs to 300,000. That discovery potentially tripled the danger, possibly shrinking the nationwide spam window to roughly 4 minutes.

In the U.S., a country of 3.8 million square miles, 340 million people are served by roughly 447,600 cell sites, and a telecom ecosystem dominated by three national carriers. There are more than 30 regional providers and hundreds of Mobile Virtual Network Operators. Illicit SIM farms are an existential threat to the system and the concept of truth.

300,000 networked phones/SIMs in the New York area — a footprint experts say could blanket every cellphone in a few minutes would enable attackers to overwhelm networks and cripple emergency channels.

This SIM farm was not the only one.

A former top federal law enforcement official told me there are others that haven't been "publicly revealed" in the Southwestern, Southeastern, and Midwestern regions of the U.S.

In short, SIM farms in the hands of bad actors could turn everyday mobile infrastructure into a scalpel for sabotage and a megaphone for lies. At this scale, the damage is fast, pervasive, and catastrophic to public safety and democratic trust.

Most dangerous of all is the disinformation it could transport.

At that speed and scale, operators could launch instant, nation-wide waves of coordinated false narratives, deepfakes, phishing and malicious links, and tailored propaganda. It would distort the news cycle, overwhelm fact-checking, and erode public trust before defenders can react. It's an unprecedented, high-velocity tool for influence and chaos that makes rapid, layered countermeasures essential.

Analysis:

Flood operations follow a predictable life cycle:

1. Seeding: A falsehood is planted in obscure or anonymous online spaces.

2. Amplification: Bots and trolls replicate and push it across multiple networks.

3. Legitimization: Influencers, politicians, or media outlets pick it up.

4. Normalization: Mainstream coverage, even when debunking, increases the footprint of the flood.

The pattern reveals where defenses fail, fact-checking happens too late, after normalization. Understanding the anatomy of "flooding the zone" helps build earlier interventions.

Takeaways:

– Falsehoods evolve through stages; intervention must happen early.

– Promoting awareness by debunking is still amplification.

– Filter first, fact-check later — don't give the lie new oxygen.

Toolkit:

• Trace narratives with tools like InVid, CrowdTangle, and Wayback Machine.

• Develop newsroom protocols for identifying emerging disinformation clusters.

• Tag and archive misleading content instead of sharing it for rebuttal.

• Coordinate with other journalists or researchers to establish timeline consistency.

Exercises

Trace the Lifecycle

Goal: Visualize the evolution of a lie.

Task: Build a four-stage timeline (seeding → amplification → legitimization → normalization) for a recent case.

Reflection: Where could you have broken the chain?

Network Overload Simulation

Goal: Practice flood triage under pressure.

Scenario: A mass SMS/Text false alert spikes nationwide. Draft your first five verified newsroom actions.

Reflection: Which step preserves public trust while you verify?

Chapter Three
What the Flood Does to Us

In late 2016, as the U.S. presidential election reached its fever pitch, a completely fake story surfaced in the darkest corners of the internet: a Washington, D.C., pizza shop was secretly running a child-trafficking ring connected to top Democratic officials. It began on obscure, sketchy message boards and then spread to reputable ones, where anonymous users traded conspiracy theories, memes, and unverified claims. Within hours, automated social media accounts, or bots programmed to amplify emotional or sensational content, began spreading the rumor across Twitter and Facebook. The claim was outrageous, but that's precisely why it thrived. A YouTube video soon appeared, weaving together random photos, dimly lit screenshots, and ominous music to create a narrative of hidden evil. Within days, fringe websites published "investigations" claiming to expose coded language in leaked emails, and the story took on the illusion of legitimacy.

The "Pizza-Gate" conspiracy theory, as it became known, was born from a toxic mix of political tribalism, digital manipulation, and a failure of basic media literacy. It emerged just weeks after WikiLeaks published hacked emails from John Podesta, Hillary Clinton's campaign chair. Conspiracy theorists falsely claimed that ordinary phrases in those emails, words like "pizza" and "cheese," were code for child exploitation. Online forums buzzed with armchair detectives connecting imaginary dots. Photos of the pizzeria's art and décor were twisted into "evidence." As the narrative spread, partisan media outlets gave it oxygen, publishing articles and videos that repeated or hinted at the allegations without any verification.

By the time credible journalists began to debunk the story, the damage was done. Millions of people had already seen, shared, or discussed the false claims. Algorithms on social media rewarded engagement, not accuracy. Every click, like, and retweet pushed the lie further into the mainstream. Influencers with large followings adopted the slogan "Save the Children," transforming a fringe fantasy into a moral crusade. For many, belief in the conspiracy became a badge of identity, proof that they were the ones who "saw through" elite corruption.

Then came the real-world consequence. On December 4, 2016, Edgar Maddison Welch, a 28-year-old man from North Carolina, drove to Washington armed with an AR-15-style rifle. Convinced he was rescuing victims of abuse, he stormed into Comet Ping Pong on Connecticut Ave. and fired several shots. He found no children, no basement, no evidence because there was none. Police arrested him within minutes. No one was injured, but the episode became a defining moment in America's understanding of how disinformation metastasizes.

"Pizza-Gate" revealed something fundamental about the modern information ecosystem: that the boundary between digital fiction and physical violence has eroded. A false narrative, once confined to the internet's fringe, can reach millions before truth has time to catch up. Each layer of amplification, from bots to bloggers to broadcasters, turns speculation into conviction. What began as a rumor on an obscure forum ended with a man pulling a trigger in a busy restaurant. The story of "Pizza-Gate" is not just about one lie; it is about how the machinery of modern disinformation can turn imagination into action and belief into danger.

Analysis:

The "flood" weaponizes confusion. Its purpose is to overload cognition and erode trust.

Psychologists call this cognitive exhaustion: when presented with too much contradictory information, people disengage. The consequences are profound:

- Civic paralysis: When "everyone lies," participation declines.

- Polarization: When facts collapse, only identity remains.

- Erosion of institutions: Courts, media, and science lose legitimacy.

This is not healthy skepticism; it's engineered despair. A demoralized public is easier to manipulate.

Takeaways:

– The flood's aim is despair, not persuasion.

– Protect people's attention — it's a shared public resource.

– Exhaustion is the enemy's greatest weapon.

Toolkit:

- Limit exposure: set information hygiene schedules — no endless scrolling.

- Train audiences to recognize emotional triggers (fear, outrage, disgust).

- Create "slow news" segments prioritizing verified information.

- Encourage communities to discuss misinformation collectively instead of privately.

Exercises

Cognitive Load Test

Goal: Feel the cost of overload.

Task: Consume a chaotic feed for 3 minutes, then write a 1 sentence summary and list three unverifiable claims you saw.

Reflection: How did fatigue change your confidence?

Emotional Trigger Mapping

Goal: Detect manipulation vectors.

Task: Collect three misleading posts; tag the primary trigger (fear, outrage, disgust, pride) and the call to action.

Reflection: Which triggers recur in your community, and why?

Chapter Four

The Thin Line Between Disinformation and Misinformation

The COVID-19 pandemic did more than strain hospitals and divide families.

In September of 2021, I did a series of reports called *COVID Conspiracy*. It exposed the razor-thin line between misinformation and disinformation—and showed how easily one can bleed into the other. In 2021, foreign actors targeted Americans with false and misleading claims about vaccines, exploiting fear, confusion, and political grievance.

At the center of it was a company called Fazze.

In May of that year, German social-media influencer Mirko Drotschmann opened an email offering him money to post negative content about U.S.-made vaccines—specifically Pfizer. The message cited CDC statistics, including the 7,899 reported deaths after vaccination recorded between December 2020 and September 2021. What the message carefully omitted was that only 0.0020% of those who'd been vaccinated had died – and that no link had been established between the vaccines and those deaths.

The script was explicit:

"Say the information is your own research.

Do not mention you are being paid.

Do not cite Fazze.

Make it look organic."

Drotschmann dug deeper and discovered Fazze wasn't just a marketing agency, it was tied to an advertising network called

ADNow, which investigative teams traced back to Moscow. The goal wasn't debate; it was destabilization. The narrative was preloaded. The influencers were simply meant to carry it forward.

This was not misinformation. This was disinformation—false, orchestrated, funded, concealed.

But on the receiving end, it didn't always look that way.

During that same timeframe, Washington, DC-area residents, including Samantha Williams, who lived in Prince George's County, received a text message with a flyer about vaccine side effects. She told me that the material was "technically true," but "inflated the risk" and exaggerated dangers in ways designed to provoke fear. It blended real data with misleading framing, transforming partial truths into a deceptive whole.

This is where the line blurs: a message that contains truth but uses truth as a weapon.

Experts told me that this hybrid content—half true, half distorted—is the most effective modern propaganda. It slips past defenses. It looks like information. It feels like concern. It spreads like wildfire. And it does the job.

Former CIA operative Robert Baer put it starkly:

"I've never seen the Soviet Union or Russia this effective in their covert action campaigns."

Retired FBI agent Tom O'Connor added:

"Russia—first off, their game is sowing polarization in the United States. Divide and conquer is their thing."

That is the heart of it. The aim was never simply to confuse Americans about vaccines. The aim was to divide them from one another, undermine trust in institutions, and push U.S. society into a deeper state of suspicion and fragmentation.

The pandemic was the battlefield. Vaccines were the vector. Americans were the target.

Disinformation doesn't always come screaming with fake stories and wild conspiracies. Often, it comes quietly camouflaged as concern, fact sheets, "just asking questions," or "research" that never shows its source. The damage is the same: people begin to doubt what's real, fear what's safe, and trust what's dangerous.

This is how a foreign disinformation campaign becomes domestic misinformation. And once it spreads from one ordinary person to another, the original intent disappears—but the impact remains.

That is the thin line.

That is the danger of the age we're living in.

Analysis:

Why This Campaign Worked: This operation succeeded because it exploited a series of vulnerabilities:

High emotion, low clarity.

Pandemics trigger fear. They are the perfect environment for manipulating perception.

Borrowed legitimacy.

False claims wrapped in legitimate data confuse readers who don't have the context to evaluate the numbers.

Distributed amplification.

Paid influencers laundered the narrative. Once it crossed into local sharing, it looked like organic grassroots concern.

Asymmetry.

It takes one click to spread a false claim. It takes expertise, time, and trust to correct one.

Hybrid content.

Fact-based framing blended with exaggeration made the message nearly immune to simple debunking.

Disinformation's greatest power is not its falseness—it is its believability.

Takeaways

- Intent is the dividing line.

Misinformation is accidental; disinformation is engineered.

- Truth can be weaponized.

A technically accurate statistic can mislead if stripped of context.

- Influencers can be modern covert assets.

Paid posts masquerading as personal opinion can shift public perception with minimal traceability.

- Foreign operations rely on domestic sharing.

Americans often become unwitting amplifiers.

- The danger is cumulative.

Each small misleading message adds friction, confusion, fear—and division.

Toolkit: How to Detect the Thin Line

Look for missing context.

If a statistic is true but its relevance is unclear, someone may be using truth to mislead.

Check the incentive.

Who benefits if you believe this? Who loses?

Watch for emotional manipulation.

Fear, outrage, uncertainty, these are early warning signs of influence operations.

Verify sponsorship.

If a post seems oddly polished, strangely phrased, or synchronized across influencers, investigate who's behind it.

Track repetition.

If the same message appears across different platforms in slightly different forms, it may be part of a coordinated effort.

Separate source from sharer.

Ask: Did the person sharing this create it? Or are they just passing it along?

Exercises:

1. Context Check

Take any public-health claim you've seen online.

A.   Identify which parts are factually true.

B.   Identify which parts lack context.

C.   Rewrite the message in a neutral way.

Notice how different it becomes.

2. Intent Mapping

Choose a misleading message you've encountered.

Create a three-column chart:

A.   What the message says

B.   Who benefits if people believe it

C.   What behavior it encourages

Patterns will emerge quickly.

3. Provenance Trace

Pick one viral claim and trace it back as far as possible.

A.   Who posted it first?

B.	Was that account real?

C.	Was the claim identical in early versions?

This exercise reveals how misinformation often starts as something else.

Part Two: Strategic Countermeasures

Chapter Five
Narrow the Firehose

A powerful World War II example of narrowing the firehose came during the Battle of Britain in 1940, when Nazi Germany launched a relentless campaign to annihilate Britain's air defenses and open the door for invasion. The Luftwaffe's strategy was rooted in volume and velocity—waves of bombers escorted by fighters poured across the Channel, day after day, an airborne firehose of destruction meant to overwhelm not just the Royal Air Force's planes, but its ability to think, plan, and respond. For Germany, the objective wasn't simply to destroy Britain's aircraft; it was to drown its defenders in chaos, forcing them to react to every feint and phantom threat until the system collapsed from exhaustion.

But Britain refused to play by those terms. Under the calm and calculating leadership of Air Chief Marshal Hugh Dowding, the RAF didn't try to match the Luftwaffe sortie for sortie. Dowding understood that reacting to every German maneuver would quickly drain his limited pool of trained pilots and aircraft. Instead, he and his team created a revolutionary command-and-control system, the first of its kind—built on information discipline. Britain's "Chain Home" radar network provided early warning of incoming raids, allowing operators to distinguish real attacks from diversions. Data from radar stations was funneled to Fighter Command headquarters at Bentley Priory, where it was visualized on vast plotting tables and verified through cross-checks from ground observers. Every signal, every radar blip, was filtered through a deliberate process designed to separate noise from threat.

This approach transformed how wars would be fought. Fighter Command didn't scramble planes at every sighting; it acted only when radar and intelligence confirmed a real target. Squadrons were deployed strategically, not reactively. Controllers directed pilots to the most dangerous incursions, conserving energy, fuel, and morale. Britain's defense became not a matter of brute force, but of cognitive clarity—a victory of signal management over information overload.

While Germany's forces relied on speed and volume to overwhelm, Dowding's network thrived on precision and restraint. Every false signal ignored, every unnecessary sortie avoided, was a small but crucial win in preserving strength. Pilots fought fewer battles, but the ones they did fight mattered more. The results spoke for themselves: despite being outnumbered nearly two to one, the RAF maintained control of British skies. In the process, it handed Hitler his first major defeat, forcing the cancellation of Operation Sea Lion, Germany's planned invasion of Britain.

The Battle of Britain was more than an air war—it was an information war. The British victory demonstrated that mastery of communication, intelligence, and selective engagement could defeat even a superior force. In essence, Britain filtered the flood. It didn't win by shouting louder, but by listening smarter. The same principle applies in today's battles over information: in a world saturated with noise, victory belongs to those who can discern truth from distraction, focus resources, and refuse to be drawn into every fight. Dowding's lesson endures: in war, as in information defense, clarity is power.

The translation of this to the modern civilian world: We're not chasing sparks — we're tracing patterns. Filter the flood and win the day.

Analysis:

Every act of coverage is an amplifier. Journalists often feel compelled to address every rumor, but this reaction fuels the flood. By consolidating, contextualizing, and reframing, reporters can minimize harm.

Toolkit:

- Bundle falsehoods into periodic "trend summaries."

- Lead with verified facts; never headline the lie.

- Use framing language: "Unverified claims circulated by anonymous sources."

- Ask: Does coverage serve the public, or the propagandist?

Takeaways:

-   Precision beats volume.

The key to resilience—whether in wartime or not, the information space is a target. Don't respond to every provocation. Focus energy on what's real, verified, and consequential.

-   Filtering is a form of strength.

Like Britain's radar system, newsrooms and institutions must build systems to detect, verify, and triage — separating genuine threats from noise. Smart restraint is a strategic weapon.

-   Don't be baited by the flood.

Disinformation thrives on emotional reactions. Refusing to chase every false alarm denies adversaries the engagement they crave.

-   Patterns reveal the plan.

By mapping recurring narratives and identifying their origins, journalists and analysts can expose manipulation at scale — not just isolated falsehoods.

-   Information discipline wins trust.

Audiences learn what to believe by observing how journalists behave under pressure. Calm, consistent, contextual coverage signals reliability and disarms the chaos merchants.

- Strategic silence is not weakness.

Choosing not to amplify is itself an act of defense. Ignoring noise protects the information environment and the public's focus from exploitation.

Exercises:

1. The False-Alarm Drill

Goal: Train reaction discipline.

Scenario: Three viral posts claim a foreign cyberattack has shut down regional airports.

Task: In a simulated newsroom setting, outline your response protocol.

A. Identify what not to do in the first 30 minutes.

B. List two trusted verification points.

C. Draft the single line your newsroom would publish while confirming facts.

D. Debrief: What emotional or editorial pressures tempted you to overreact?

2. The Radar Table

Goal: Practice pattern detection.

Task: Collect five recent misinformation stories. Chart the topic, source, amplification network, and emotional trigger.

Objective: Spot the repeating themes; fear, identity, and outrage that connect them.

Lesson: Once patterns emerge, coverage can shift from reactive to analytical.

NOTES

Chapter Six
Pre-bunking Instead of Debunking

Shift from reaction to prevention. The best way to stop disinformation is to warn before the wave. Audiences primed for manipulation are far less likely to fall for it. Pre-bunking inoculates. It teaches people how lies work before they see them. It's not about censorship; it's about mental immunity. The most powerful defenses are built before the attack begins. Google's Jigsaw team proved this in 2022–24 with short YouTube ads that showed viewers how propaganda works: scapegoating, emotional manipulation, and false dilemmas. Those who saw the clips were 29% less likely to believe false stories later. Finland went even further, embedding media literacy into school curricula after years of Russian disinformation. Students learn to dissect propaganda the way others learn grammar. The result: Finland now ranks at or near the top in Europe for resilience to fake news. Awareness before exposure builds lasting cognitive immunity.

Map Recurring Narratives

Disinformation rarely invents something new. It recycles the same storylines: election fraud, migrant "invasions," and cultural "collapse." Mapping these recurring myths lets journalists and analysts see the next wave before it breaks. Ukraine's Center for Strategic Communications mastered this before Russia's 2022 invasion, publicly forecasting that Moscow would accuse Kyiv of shelling civilians before attacking. When those exact claims appeared online, the warning had already blunted their impact. The U.S. Cybersecurity and Infrastructure Security Agency (CISA) had used the same principle in 2020 with its "Rumor Control" page, which listed likely false election claims in advance. Pattern recognition beats panic.

Use Visual Inoculation

Disinformation spreads through what people see—not just what they read. That's why effective pre-bunking must be visual. Taiwan's "Humor Over Rumor" campaign used memes and humor to parody Chinese propaganda before it spread, transforming fear into laughter. During the COVID-19 pandemic, the World Health Organization pre-bunked misinformation with infographics showing how fake cures and conspiracy networks spread. These visuals didn't just explain manipulation; they revealed its mechanics. When people can see how deception works, they're far less likely to be deceived by it.

Shift from Reaction to Prevention

Debunking is reactive. It's an endless cleanup effort. Pre-bunking is proactive. It builds cognitive firebreaks before the spark. The BBC Africa Eye project put this into action during African elections, training young voters to recognize fake videos and rumors on social media before they appeared. Those who took part were half as likely to believe the false stories later. Across Europe, EUvsDisinfo, a team of EU government experts fighting disinformation, issues advance alerts on Kremlin narratives ahead of major political events, helping newsrooms prepare. In Indonesia, civil society groups used AI ahead of the 2024 election to predict deepfakes and warn voters early. These are the front lines of prevention—faster, cheaper, and far more effective than chasing lies after they spread.

The Principle

Debunking is mopping up after the flood. Pre-bunking builds the dam. A public that expects to be manipulated is far harder to fool. The next stage of information defense is not reaction, but readiness to forewarn, teaching citizens not what to think, but how to see the manipulation coming.

Analysis:

Pre-bunking inoculates minds by exposing audiences to weak versions of manipulative techniques. Like vaccination, it builds cognitive immunity. By contrast, debunking acts too late, after belief forms.

Takeaways:

– It's easier to prevent belief than reverse it.

– Expose tactics, not just lies.

– Preparedness outperforms correction.

– Debunking works, but pre-bunking is more effective.

Toolkit:

• Issue pre-bunk alerts before major events.

• Develop lesson plans using sample fakes.

• Share "warning signals" — language patterns, emotional hooks, and tactics.

• Encourage critical curiosity: ask, "Who benefits if I believe this?"

Exercises:

Design a Pre-bunk Alert

Goal: Shift from reaction to prevention.

Task: Draft a 60 word pre-bunk for an upcoming event, naming the likely tactic and a verification step for audiences.

Reflection: How does tone reduce panic while informing?

Predict the Narrative

Goal: Anticipate recycled myths.

Scenario: For the same event, list two likely false narratives and a visual you'll use to inoculate.

Reflection: What early signals tipped you off?

Chapter Seven

Collective Defense — A NATO for Journalism

On the morning of September 11, 2001, at 9:50 a.m., I stood on the roof of the Voice of America headquarters in Washington, DC, where I worked at the time. From that rooftop, I could see thick, black plumes of smoke rising from the Pentagon, almost two miles away, curling into a crystal-blue sky that only moments earlier had been perfectly clear. Flames, supercharged by jet fuel, clawed at the edges of the nerve center of American defense. The air smelled of burning metal and chaos. I did not yet know that another plane—United Airlines Flight 93—was still in the air, hijacked and heading toward Washington.

Later, we would learn that its likely target was the U.S. Capitol, a gleaming white dome just across the street from the VOA building—barely more than two hundred yards away. If not for the extraordinary courage of the passengers and crew who fought back, forcing the aircraft down in a field in Shanksville, Pennsylvania, the attack could have decapitated America's democracy. Forty-four people died on that flight. But their sacrifice saved countless others, including those of us standing on the roof of the VOA in stunned disbelief that morning.

That day everything changed. It shattered illusions of safety, rewired how the world understood security, and ushered in a new era of vigilance and vulnerability. For the first and only time in its history, the North Atlantic Treaty Organization invoked Article Five—the collective defense clause that declares an attack on one member is an attack on all. Allies stood shoulder to shoulder with the United States. In the smoke and sorrow of that morning, I saw not only destruction, but the birth of a new kind of global unity—one forged in grief, resolve, and the shared determination never to let such darkness prevail again.

Article 5 reads as follows:

"The Parties agree that an armed attack against one or more of them in Europe or North America shall be considered an attack against them all and consequently they agree that, if such an armed attack occurs, each of them, in exercise of the right of individual or collective self-defence recognised by Article 51 of the Charter of the United Nations, will assist the Party or Parties so attacked by taking forthwith, individually and in concert with the other Parties, such action as it deems necessary, including the use of armed force, to restore and maintain the security of the North Atlantic area."

That is the foundation of NATO's collective defense mandate. Journalists need to make the same kind of pact to defend each other, minus the use of armed force. If one journalist is unfairly attacked, marginalized, and actively loses their ability to do their work, other journalists should step in and assist them.

I call this idea NATO4NEWS. On October 28, 2025, at the European External Action Service's Connecting Media Conference in Brussels, I brought this idea up to the 85 journalists, fact checkers, and content creators from 62 countries in attendance. Not only was there overwhelming support for it, but a new, unprecedented avenue for collaboration in the fight against disinformation was opened.

Analysis:

Disinformation thrives when it isolates its targets. A united network of journalists sharing threat data can blunt coordinated campaigns. Collective defense builds resilience across borders.

Takeaways:

– The flood isolates; solidarity neutralizes.

– An attack on one outlet is an attack on all.

– Truth spreads faster when shared.

Toolkit:

• Form regional newsroom alliances for disinformation monitoring.

• Share data via secure channels (Signal, encrypted cloud).

• Create unified editorial standards for covering falsehoods.

• Use real-time dashboards to detect cross-border narrative shifts.

Exercises:

Build a NATO4News Pact

Goal: Formalize collective defense of journalists.

Task: Write a one paragraph mutual aid protocol: verification channel, legal triage, platform escalation, and support messaging.

Reflection: Consider how this would benefit your team today?

Rapid-Response Drill

Goal: Reduce time to truth.

Scenario: A colleague is swarmed by bots. In 10 minutes, outline "verify support report" steps and assign roles.

Reflection: Which move most limits amplification?

Part Three: Building Resilience

Chapter Eight

Clarity Beats Clutter

Disinformation feeds on confusion. It floods the space with so much noise that people stop trying to separate fact from fiction. The best defense isn't more data—it's clarity. Short, repeated framing cuts through chaos more effectively than a thousand-word rebuttal.

New Zealand's response to the COVID-19 pandemic became a global model of this principle. Prime Minister Jacinda Ardern's daily briefings used a calm, simple refrain: "Stay home. Save lives. Be kind." Those six words carried science, empathy, and national unity better than any chart. They became a rallying point, a shared code of behavior in a sea of uncertainty. Clarity doesn't simplify the truth; it amplifies it. When information is consistent, concise, and repeated, it builds resilience faster than fear can spread.

Say It Simply

Every false claim doesn't deserve a debate. In fact, long refutations often make things worse by repeating the lie. The most effective counter is direct and confident: "This is false. Here's the fact."

That's exactly how the Associated Press and Reuters tackled online falsehoods during the 2020 U.S. election. They turned traditional fact checks into quick, visual "truth cards" designed for fast sharing. Each one named the lie, corrected it in a single sentence, and provided verifiable evidence—nothing more. Their tone was firm, not emotional. Their design was clean, not cluttered, and audiences responded. Engagement rates spiked, particularly among readers fatigued by outrage and argument. The lesson: simplicity is not weakness. It's precision under pressure.

Storytelling Matters

Data informs the mind, but story moves the heart. Disinformation spreads because it feels like a story, full of villains, victims, and drama. The truth can win only if it learns to speak in that same emotional register.

Public health campaigns in Ghana and Chicago proved the point during the vaccine rollout. Instead of citing percentages or medical jargon, they shared first-person videos of neighbors, parents, and pastors explaining why they got vaccinated. A grandmother's quiet pride carried more weight than a government spokesman's statistics.

The BBC's "Disinformation Diaries" applied this principle to investigative journalism. Rather than listing falsehoods, the series followed real people who had been misled—and traced how they found their way back to the truth. The narrative form made facts memorable because it made them human. People remember stories, not spreadsheets.

Use Trusted Messengers

The truth must come from voices people already trust. It's not enough to be right; the messenger must be credible in the audience's eyes. That's why disinformation campaigns work through familiar faces—local influencers, community figures, even friends. Countering them requires the same understanding of human trust networks.

In Finland, this insight became national policy. The country's "Media Literacy Defenders" program trains librarians, teachers, and clergy to detect and defuse misinformation inside their own communities. When a falsehood starts to circulate, it's not a distant government agency that responds—it's a local voice speaking the local dialect of trust. The result: Finland consistently ranks as one of the most resilient democracies against fake news.

The same approach worked in Arizona's 2022 midterm elections. Instead of relying on federal messaging, county election officials brought pastors, veterans, and professors onto local radio and livestreams to explain how ballots were counted. When people heard it from someone they knew, the conspiracy theories lost their sting.

Truth needs allies who can carry it into the places institutions can't reach. In an era when people believe those they know more than those in power, trust is the delivery system for clarity.

Clarity is the countermeasure to chaos. The most effective communicators don't try to outshout the flood. They out-focus it. Say it simply, tell it as a story, and let trusted voices carry it forward. Disinformation's power lies in confusion. Truth's power lies in precision, repetition, and humanity.

In this war of noise, clarity isn't just good communication; it's a form of defense.

Analysis:

Disinformation thrives on clutter; clarity cuts through it. Short, disciplined framing strengthens memory and keeps audiences oriented toward verified facts. Clarity is not dumbing down. It's focus.

Takeaways:

– Clarity is the ultimate filter.

– Precision persuades where volume fails.

– Simple = memorable.

Toolkit:

• Develop a one-sentence truth frame for every complex story.

• Lead with the verified core; move context below.

• Test clarity — ask a non-expert to restate your message.

- Repeat key phrases for reinforcement; consistency beats novelty.

Exercises:

Clarity Sprint

Goal: Cut through clutter.

Task: Turn a complex policy into one crisp sentence, then a 15-second read for radio.

Reflection: What detail did you cut that didn't change the truth?

Trusted Messenger Map

Goal: Route truth through trust.

Task: List five local messengers and the audiences they reach; match each to a message about your beat.

Reflection: How will you brief them during crises?

Chapter Nine

Tech & Platforms — Turning Down the Volume

The Counter Extremism Project (CEP), founded by former U.S. Ambassador Mark Wallace, former Homeland Security Advisor Fran Townsend, and former Senator Joseph Lieberman, became one of the first organizations to expose how extremist and disinformation networks were being amplified and monetized by the world's largest tech platforms. Their researchers uncovered a brutal truth: algorithms rewarded outrage because outrage paid. The more divisive or shocking the content, the longer users stayed engaged — and the more ads they saw. That engagement loop became a business model, not a bug.

When brands discovered their ads appearing beside terrorist propaganda, conspiracy theories, and hate speech, the backlash was immediate. Corporate giants like AT&T, Verizon, and PepsiCo yanked their advertising budgets. Platforms panicked. Google tightened its ad policies and launched the Redirect Method to steer users away from extremist material. Facebook and Twitter adopted tools to detect and block extremist uploads. The noise dropped — not because truth won, but because profit noticed.

Dr. Hans-Jakob Schindler, senior director at the Counter Extremism Project, underscored this in multiple conversations with me on The Hunt (WTOP Radio). "Big-tech platforms are not neutral utilities," he warned. "They are amplifiers with profit incentives. Unless those incentives are realigned, extremists and state actors will keep using their systems faster than governments can react." His point was piercingly clear: the danger lies not only in the content itself, but in the structure that monetizes it.

In 2020, the Stop Hate for Profit campaign demonstrated how pressure on revenue could drive reform. More than 750 major advertisers — from Coca-Cola and Unilever to Ben & Jerry's — paused spending on Facebook to protest its tolerance for hate and misinformation. Meta promised policy changes and greater transparency, though many critics dismissed them as superficial. Still, for the first time, disinformation carried a measurable financial penalty.

After the sale of X (formerly Twitter) in 2022, it became a live case study in the same dynamic. As hate speech and conspiracy content surged, major advertisers fled. Transparency reports reappeared, lawsuits followed, and Wall Street noticed. The message was unmistakable: advertisers, not algorithms, hold the real power dial.

Grassroots activism magnified the pressure. Campaigns like Sleeping Giants in the U.S. and Stop Funding Hate in the U.K. mobilized citizens to contact companies whose ads appeared on sites promoting racism and division. Every dollar withdrawn from a toxic platform made falsehoods less profitable.

Finally, Europe translated outrage into law. The Digital Services Act (DSA) forced major platforms to disclose how they rank, recommend, and monetize content — making secrecy expensive and accountability unavoidable. For the first time, governments began regulating not just what platforms publish, but how they profit. In doing so, the DSA reframed the fight against disinformation: truth can't win by persuasion alone — it must also compete on the balance sheet.

Analysis:

Algorithms reward outrage because outrage drives profit. But the same systems can be tuned for authenticity, transparency, and accountability if public pressure and regulation align.

Takeaways:

– What lies earn, transparency erodes.

– Platforms can decide whether truth is presented or not.

– Economic incentives often shape truth's reach.

Toolkit:

• Demand algorithmic transparency reports from platforms.

• Track coordinated inauthentic behavior and document takedowns.

• Push advertisers to block disinformation domains.

• Support laws requiring AI-generated content labeling and data provenance.

Exercises:

Ad Pressure Audit

Goal: Align incentives with integrity.

Task: Pick one brand and one platform. Check if the brand's ads appear beside disinformation; draft a 3 line outreach note.

Reflection: What data would persuade the brand to act?

Algorithm Watch

Goal: Observe engagement bias.

Task: Track a topic across two platforms for 7 days, logging which content gets boosted.

Reflection: What can be done to curb the bias?

NOTES

Chapter Ten

Audience Resilience & Media Literacy

When I spoke to him in early October of 2025, former CIA and NSA Director, retired Air Force General Michael Hayden, was deeply concerned. "Disinformation," he warned, "is eroding America from within and warping our alliances abroad." His voice carried the weight of someone who had seen firsthand how truth, or the absence of it, can shape the fate of nations. "The only antidote," he said, "is an unapologetic return to truth over spin, stated plainly, even when it's politically inconvenient."

Hayden's words landed with particular force because he is not a pundit or partisan; he's a man who spent decades navigating the shadows where facts and deception constantly collide. As CIA director during some of America's most turbulent years in the fight against terrorism, and earlier as head of the National Security Agency, Hayden helped build systems designed to protect the nation from external threats. But what unsettled him most when we spoke was an internal one: a nation losing its capacity to discern reality from fiction.

He described a country where citizens increasingly "don't know the truth," where information overload and ideological echo chambers have made objective facts almost optional. "The trend line for truth," Hayden said, "is going down, down, down." The general who once oversaw global intelligence networks now sees the erosion of civic intelligence at home as the most dangerous front in America's modern security struggle.

Hayden's remedy was both urgent and practical: rebuild civic literacy from the ground up. He believes that every American child should be trained—starting in elementary school—to ask a single, powerful question: "Is that true or not true?" This, he argued, is not merely about education policy but about national survival. "A citizenry that can't tell fact from fiction can't defend a democracy," he said. The goal isn't to turn students into cynics, but into critical thinkers capable of navigating the flood of manipulated narratives that now define modern life.

His experience makes him a credible messenger. In 2018, after the arrest of Russian agent Maria Butina, Hayden noted that modern espionage is less about stealing secrets than about manipulating perceptions—the very terrain where disinformation thrives. Years earlier, following the Snowden leaks, he warned that the exposure of U.S. surveillance programs had crippled the intelligence community's ability to detect foreign actors operating in the digital space. He spoke then about how quickly adversaries adapt once they understand the architecture of truth and secrecy—a warning that now applies not just to spies, but to societies.

When Hayden calls for truth to reclaim its place in public life, it isn't nostalgia—it's strategy. He said Americans must once again demand that intelligence and national-security professionals present facts without political interference and insist that presidents and policymakers act on what is real, not what is convenient. The corrosion of truth, he warned, doesn't just weaken debate; it weakens defense.

Hayden's message to U.S. leaders is unmistakable: make truth—not spin—the guiding principle again, or risk watching the nation's democratic capacity to think, decide, and defend itself collapse under a flood of manufactured falsehoods. In an age of digital deception, he believes civic literacy is not just education—it is America's last line of defense.

Analysis:

An aware public is disinformation's kryptonite. Teaching verification skills at the community level builds cultural immunity and restores shared standards of evidence.

Takeaways:

- Media literacy is civic defense.
- Verification before virality.
- Trust grows where truth is visible.

Toolkit:

-Host community truth nights in libraries, schools, and congregations.

-Encourage radical transparency — show your receipts, link your data.

- Collaborate with educators to embed media literacy across curricula.

Exercises:

Community Truth Lab

Goal: Practice verification in public.

Task: Host a 30 minute session: participants bring one claim; you run them through the Five Step Check (Pause → Source → Reverse Search → Verify → Share).

Reflection: Afterward, assess which step did audiences find hardest?

Five-Step Fact-Check Drill (Expanded)

Goal: Make verification habitual.

Task: Run two current claims through the five steps; publish a short post with proof. Include links and images.

Reflection: What template will you reuse weekly?

NOTES

Part Four:

The Road Ahead | Flood 2.0 and Beyond

Chapter Eleven
Belarus and the Making of an Alternate Reality

It's a rainy, chilly day in Brussels in late October 2025. I sit down for an interview with Belarusian exile Natalia Belikova, C.E.O. of Press Club Belarus, in between sessions of the European Union's EEAS Connecting Media Conference.

Her tone is calm and deliberate, but the story she tells is chilling. I ask her to explain the evolution of disinformation in Belarus. She explains that simply distorting facts is no longer what they do. "We are talking about crafting an entirely alternative reality," she says.

In Belarus, falsehood isn't random — it's structural. "It's an entire system that works to create an alternative reality in the minds of people," she says. "TV, radio, print, and also digital now — they all work for the one purpose: to create the reality that the government wants you to have. And there is no alternative."

This is not censorship; it's replacement. "What Belarusian propaganda is doing, and doing quite successfully," Belikova explains, "is replacing the true meaning of words." Democracy no longer means institutions or choice. "Democracy is how you show your patriotism," she says. "Elections are the way to show you support the government." Even "human rights" and "terrorism" have been redefined to serve power. In that fog, she says, "Truth isn't refuted — it's dissolved."

But Belarusians still sense the cracks. "People really see the discrepancy between what the authorities say — that salaries are going up — and what life they're actually living." Despite banned polling and state control, many "try to get information from a variety of sources."

The breaking point came after the 2020 elections

A group of IT experts built an app to prove the vote was rigged. "The evidence was clear," Belikova says. "People went into the streets — and on the third day, the authorities started sweeping, arresting people everywhere, torturing them in prison." When independent media reported the brutality, "the country was in shock."

"Within half a year," she says, "we went from being more or less free to one of the most repressed countries in Europe." An estimated one million people fled — "not just journalists, but doctors, teachers, engineers, lawyers." Independent outlets were crushed overnight. "They closed the largest portal within one day... and the archives of twenty years were lost."

The regime sustains itself through fear and dependency. "They built the system for many years," she explains. "Loyalty and obeying any order is the key." Police recruits are screened for "relatives with free minds." Those who are hired are bound by incentives: "You get cheaper credits to buy apartments. Once you're there, you cannot quit... even if you want."

Her warning to the West is direct. "We in Belarus always believed American institutions were the true ones," she says. "But it's alarming to watch this system apparently not working as it should." When institutions become hollow, she cautions, "it is very easy to overtake them." Her plea is simple: "Any legal way is a good way... using the power of law and the rule of law to make institutions work again."

Then her composure breaks. "I haven't seen my family since 2019. My father is dying in hospital, and I cannot go and say goodbye to him." Her eyes become glassy with tears, and her voice trembles, but steadies again. "If my kids ever ask what Belarus is, I want to tell them I did everything I could."

Sadly a few days later, her father passed away.

Flood 2.0 is not about falsehoods — it's about the capture of reality itself. Belarus shows how news becomes ritual, and language a weapon. Belikova's message to the world is clear: Guard the words. Guard the institutions. Guard the people who still tell the truth.

Analysis:

AI enables hyper-personalized disinformation tailored to your fears and habits. Synthetic voices, faces, and text can fabricate events faster than newsrooms can verify them. This isn't about lying — it's about manufacturing perception.

Takeaways:

– Flood 2.0 fabricates reality itself.

– The future of truth is technical and moral.

– Filtering the future means defending perception.

Toolkit:

See the seams - Train journalists and analysts to spot anomalies — odd eye-blinks, mismatched shadows, warped consonants. Tools like InVID and Microsoft's authenticator can help.

Secure the chain of custody - Adopt provenance standards like the Content Authenticity Initiative (CAI) and C2PA, which tag legitimate media with verifiable metadata.

Build rapid-response teams - Cross-sector coalitions — newsrooms, tech firms, regulators — must act within minutes when synthetic media goes viral.

Teach deepfake hygiene - Public skepticism saves lives. Verify before sharing. Treat every "too-perfect" clip with suspicion.

Exercises:

Deepfake Spotter

Goal: Build detection instincts.

Task: Evaluate three suspect clips; note artifacts (blinks, lighting, phoneme lip sync, reflections) and provenance gaps.

Reflection: Which artifact was most reliable?

Reality Capture Drill

Goal: Verify perception under speed.

Scenario: A viral image drives panic. Use reverse search, geolocation, and weather/time cues to verify.

Reflection: What chain of custody practice will you adopt?

Conclusion

Playing the Long Game

In late October of 2025, at the Connecting Media Conference in Brussels, Belgium, which was organized by the European Union's EEAS, while listening to some of the participants in a panel discussion, a thought occurred to me.

The battle between truth and lies will never end.

Everyday babies are born with clean, beautiful, brains. Aside from the behavior and decisions of their mothers, they will have been mostly untouched by the world they're entering. As they grow up, they will be shaped by their physical environments, and psychologically, by the people they interact with, the stories they hear and read, and the physical experiences they themselves have. All will have to decide what and who to believe; and what to do about their beliefs. Unfortunately, there will always be people and organizations seeking to influence them with messages supporting or promoting something that is less than 100% true, and that may cause either mental or physical harm. And in this age, when electronic devices carry messages at unprecedented speeds, they may struggle to find a way forward. If that struggle becomes too complicated, they may give up and slip into a dark place they can't find their way out of.

That is why this handbook exists. Because the danger is no longer simply that bad actors spread lies, it is that the velocity, precision, and volume of those lies now overwhelm the average citizen's ability to discern reality. In such a world, truth does not survive on its own; it must be protected, tended, defended. And the responsibility for that defense does not belong only to governments or institutions but to every one of us who cares about the health of our democracies, the safety of our families, and the clarity of our own minds. Fighting disinformation is not a technical chore. It is a civic obligation. It is a form of national service. It is, at its core, an act of moral courage.

In this moment, we are called to do more than simply recognize the threat, we are called to rise to it. For the forces that weaponize falsehood are not standing still, they are innovating, adapting, and striking at the very foundations of how people understand the world. They exploit fear, confusion, exhaustion, and the human desire for simple answers to complex problems. And if we allow the architects of deception to define our reality, they will define our destiny. This is why we cannot be passive consumers of information or silent witnesses to the corrosion of truth. We must become active stewards of clarity, people who question, verify, challenge, and refuse to surrender their judgment to the loudest voice or the fastest lie. The defense of truth begins not with institutions, but with individuals who choose to see clearly when others look away.

And so, as you step out of these pages and back into the noise of the world, remember what is at stake. Lies are not simply distortions of fact; they are assaults on freedom, agency, and human dignity. Truth, on the other hand, is the only force that can anchor a society against the tide of manipulation and fear. Yet truth does not impose itself. It must be taught, reinforced, and lived. But it's important to remember that we can't order people to do anything and expect they will willingly do it. We need to do it in a way that gives them agency. Alexander Pope wrote centuries ago, a warning that still rings with urgency today. "Men must be taught as if you taught them not; and things unknown proposed as things forgot." Let this be our charge: to seek, teach, illuminate, and to defend truth with ingenuity, humility, and resolve, especially when everything around us is lying to us.

Analysis:

Here's a central truth about the modern information environment: disinformation now moves faster than most people can think, verify, or defend themselves, creating a constant threat to personal agency, public safety, and democratic stability. The danger lies not only in the falsehoods themselves but in the erosion of society's ability to tell truth from manipulation. Protecting truth is no longer the job of institutions alone. It is a shared civic responsibility that requires active, intentional engagement and a commitment to empowering people rather than ordering them. Defending truth is an act of moral courage.

Takeaways:

-The struggle between truth and lies is permanent and each new generation enters it without preparation unless guided with intention.

-The scale, speed, and precision of modern disinformation overwhelm ordinary people who are simply trying to make sense of their world.

-Truth requires active defense from every individual, not only from institutions.

-Resilience comes from empowerment, not pressure. People resist manipulation when they feel agency.

-Defending truth is a civic and moral commitment that is essential to democracy and personal freedom.

Toolkit: How to Fight Disinformation and Stand for Truth

- Pause and verify before believing, sharing, or reacting. Delay is a form of protection.

- Trace claims to their origins by asking who is making the claim and who benefits if it spreads.

- Keep a personal list of trusted sources with proven records of accuracy and return to them during moments of uncertainty.

- Cross-check important claims with multiple independent and credible sources.

- Learn the common signs of manipulation, including emotional triggers, urgency, anonymity, lack of sourcing, selective editing, and claims of secret knowledge.

- Build cognitive immunity by regularly exposing yourself to vetted information, fact-checking tools, and critical thinking practices.

- When correcting falsehoods, approach others with respect and empathy rather than accusation.

- Make accurate information easy for others to understand and share. Use clear, simple language and accessible formats.

- Audit your information environment by removing sources of rage-bait, manipulation, and distortion.

- Model disciplined, responsible information behavior for others, including younger generations who are still forming their understanding of the world.

Exercises:

Reflection:

Write a short paragraph about a time when you believed something that later turned out to be false. Identify what made the claim convincing and what you could have checked more carefully.

Source Check:

Take a viral news story from social media and trace it back to its original source. Note how many steps, edits, or reinterpretations occurred along the way.

Manipulation Markers:

Review ten posts from your preferred social platform and identify which ones use emotional triggers, urgency, outrage, or incomplete information to influence you.

Audit Your Feed:

Spend ten minutes removing or muting accounts that routinely share unverified content, outrage-driven posts, or misleading claims. Afterward, describe how the tone of your feed changes.

Teach It Forward:

Explain one of the toolkit practices to a friend or family member using simple language. Reflect on how teaching the concept reinforces your own mastery of it.

Appendices & Quick Reference

Glossary

Algorithmic Transparency — Disclosure of how digital platforms rank, recommend, and remove content. Essential for holding technology companies accountable for the spread of disinformation.

Amplification — The deliberate or algorithmic boosting of information—true or false—through repetition, automation, or emotional appeal to expand reach and influence.

Analysis — The section in each chapter that distills lessons and identifies structural patterns behind disinformation tactics.

Battle of Britain — The 1940 air campaign in which Britain's Royal Air Force "narrowed the firehose," focusing defenses on verified threats rather than false alarms—a model for modern information discipline.

Botnet — A network of automated or semi-automated social-media accounts used to flood platforms with content, distort engagement metrics, and manipulate perception.

Collective Defense — The principle, inspired by NATO's Article 5, that journalists must defend one another when attacked or targeted for doing their jobs.

Contextualization — The act of framing facts within a verified context so audiences can interpret information without distortion.

CrowdTangle — A Meta-owned analytics tool that tracks how stories, posts, and links spread across Facebook and Instagram.

Cyber Warfare — State-sponsored or criminal activity that uses digital systems to disrupt, manipulate, or influence targets.

Deepfake — AI-generated synthetic video, image, or audio content designed to impersonate reality or discredit real individuals.

Disinformation — False or misleading information deliberately created to deceive or manipulate people, often for political, financial, or strategic gain.

Exhaustion Weaponization — A strategy of overwhelming audiences with nonstop falsehoods so they give up distinguishing truth from lies.

Fact-Checking — The process of independently verifying information using credible sources before publication or broadcast.

Filter the Zone — The book's central principle: applying disciplined focus to separate verified truth from noise and manipulation.

Flood the Zone — A tactic of saturating the information environment with contradictory or low-quality material to drown out facts and exhaust audiences.

Firehose of Falsehood — A high-volume propaganda method relying on repetition, speed, and contradiction rather than consistency or evidence.

Hybrid Warfare — The blending of conventional military operations with cyberattacks, psychological manipulation, and disinformation to weaken opponents without open conflict.

Lockdown Mode — An advanced mobile-device security setting that limits exposure to spyware and phishing attacks.

Misinformation — Factual information used maliciously, such as leaking private data or selectively framing truth to cause harm.

Media Literacy — The ability to critically evaluate news, identify bias or manipulation, and verify information authenticity.

NATO (North Atlantic Treaty Organization) — A defense alliance whose Article 5 "collective defense" clause inspired NATO4News, the model for mutual protection among journalists.

NATO4News — The author's proposal for a journalist-to-journalist solidarity network that responds collectively to disinformation attacks or suppression efforts.

Normalization — The process through which repeated falsehoods or propaganda become accepted as ordinary truth.

Open-Source Intelligence (OSINT) — The collection and verification of publicly available information—social posts, satellite images, metadata—to expose or counter disinformation.

Pre-bunking — The act of warning audiences about manipulative tactics before they encounter them, building mental resistance to deception.

Propaganda — Coordinated communication designed to shape public perception toward a political objective, often through selective truth or emotional manipulation.

Radical Transparency — The practice of showing audiences the methods, data, and sources behind reporting to build durable trust.

Resilience — The capacity of individuals or institutions to withstand manipulation, maintain trust, and recover quickly after disinformation attacks.

SIM Farm — A network of linked SIM cards or phones capable of flooding telecommunications systems, spreading false messages, or simulating mass engagement.

Strategic Silence — The deliberate editorial choice to ignore falsehoods to prevent amplification.

Synthetic Media — AI-produced video, audio, or text that mimics authentic media but may be fabricated.

Takeaways — The concise lessons at the end of each chapter summarizing defense principles and strategic insights.

Toolkit — The practical list of tools, methods, or resources following each analysis section, designed for real-world application.

Troll Farm — An organized group, often paid, that posts inflammatory or deceptive content online to provoke outrage or manipulate narratives.

Verification — The journalistic process of confirming accuracy, authenticity, and source reliability before publication.

Wayback Machine — A digital archive that preserves past versions of web pages, allowing verification of altered or deleted content.

NOTES

Newsroom Guidelines

Verification and Accuracy

• Don't quote lies in headlines.

• Lead with verified facts — make truth the frame, not the correction.

• Attribute every claim with transparent sourcing ("according to verified records…").

• Confirm every visual and video through metadata, reverse search, and provenance tools before publishing.

• Maintain a digital chain of custody for all user-generated content.

Framing and Context

• Report on tactics, not just content — explain how disinformation spreads.

• Bundle disinformation examples into trend or context reports; never amplify one falsehood in isolation.

• Headline the verified event, not the controversy.

• Provide proportional coverage: avoid giving fringe narratives equal weight to factual reporting.

• Always clarify intent — distinguish between misinformation (mistake), disinformation (malice), and malinformation (weaponized truth).

Transparency and Trust

• Show receipts — link to documents, transcripts, and primary sources whenever possible.

• Note what you don't know; uncertainty honestly stated builds credibility.

• Include a "how we verified this" box for complex investigations.

• Use radical transparency: show your process, not just your product.

• Disclose any editorial corrections or updates in visible, time-stamped notes.

Speed and Restraint

• In breaking situations, publish what is known and label what is unconfirmed.

• Resist the urge to fill the gap before facts arrive; silence can be strategic.

• Avoid reactive coverage — don't feed the firehose; filter it.

• Prioritize clarity over immediacy: better to be late and right than first and wrong.

Security and Collective Defense

• Coordinate with trusted journalists when targeted by coordinated harassment.

• Use encrypted channels (Signal, ProtonMail) for sensitive coordination.

• Enable two-factor authentication and Lockdown Mode on all work devices.

• Practice collective defense: if one journalist is attacked, others amplify verified work and correct lies.

• Share threat intelligence across borders and beats.

Ethics and Accountability

• Apply the same scrutiny to your own newsroom's assumptions as to others.'

• Avoid false equivalence — disinformation is not "just another perspective."

• Protect sources while preventing their exploitation by influence networks.

• When quoting propaganda or extremist speech, clearly frame it as such.

• Never embed disinformation images or videos without visible warning labels.

Engagement and Education

• Use social platforms to explain journalism, not argue it.

• Treat every correction as a teaching moment — "Here's how this rumor spread, and here's what's true."

• Partner with educators, librarians, and civic groups to build audience resilience.

• Publish explainers on verification tools to help the public become your ally.

• Encourage constructive audience feedback — transparency earns trust.

Long-Term Resilience

• Archive key disinformation case studies for newsroom training.

• Conduct quarterly "fire drills" simulating information crises.

• Keep a standing contact list of independent fact-checkers and platform liaisons.

• Evaluate coverage impact post-publication: did your framing reduce or amplify noise?

• Remember: every story is a chance to model discipline under pressure — and to make truth visible.

Resources

Training & Education

First Draft — Field-leading training and research on misinformation detection, verification, and digital forensics.

News Literacy Project — Classroom and community programs teaching critical news consumption and fact-checking skills.

IREX Learn to Discern — Practical training for educators and journalists to build media resilience.

UNESCO Media and Information Literacy (MIL) Toolkit — Global education resources for media-literacy curricula.

Media Literacy Now — U.S.-based advocacy group integrating media literacy into school policy and curriculum.

Poynter Institute / IFCN (International Fact-Checking Network) — Standards, certification, and training for global fact-checkers.

Fact-Checking Networks & Research Hubs

EUvsDisinfo (European External Action Service) — Monitors and exposes pro-Kremlin disinformation campaigns.

Center for European Policy Analysis (CEPA) – StratCom Program — Strategic communications and information defense research.

Graphika — Network analysis and visualization of disinformation ecosystems.

Bellingcat — Investigative collective specializing in open-source intelligence (OSINT) and digital verification.

Snopes / PolitiFact / FactCheck.org — Leading independent fact-checkers.

The Global Disinformation Index (GDI) — Research on monetization of misinformation and media-risk scoring.

Technology & Verification Tools

InVID & WeVerify — Browser plug-ins for video and image verification.

Hoaxy & Botometer (Indiana University Observatory on Social Media) — Tools to visualize and quantify bot activity.

CrowdTangle (Meta) — Social-media monitoring for journalists and researchers.

Wayback Machine / Internet Archive — Historical snapshots of deleted or altered content.

NewsGuard — Browser extension rating news and information sites for reliability.

C2PA & Content Authenticity Initiative (CAI) — Metadata standards for verifying content provenance.

Google Fact Check Explorer — Aggregates global fact-checking work for rapid searches.

Policy, Law & Advocacy

NATO StratCom COE (Strategic Communications Centre of Excellence) — Research and training on hybrid threats.

Atlantic Council – Digital Forensic Research Lab (DFRLab) — Analysis of online influence operations.

Brookings Institution / Center for Security and Emerging Technology (CSET) — Policy frameworks for AI and disinformation.

G7 Rapid Response Mechanism (RRM) — Intergovernmental coordination against foreign information manipulation.

European Digital Media Observatory (EDMO) — Cross-sector cooperation on data, disinformation, and media literacy.

Coalition for Content Provenance and Authenticity (C2PA) — Technical standards for digital content traceability.

Community & Civil Society

Stop Funding Hate / Sleeping Giants — Grassroots advertiser accountability movements.

Trust Project — Transparency standards adopted by major global news outlets.

Free Press Unlimited — Support and safety initiatives for journalists under threat.

Committee to Protect Journalists (CPJ) — Defense of press freedom and journalist safety worldwide.

Reporters Without Borders (RSF) — Global ranking and advocacy for press freedom.

INDEX

AI-generated, 8, 47, 66
algorithm, 12
algorithms, 11, 1, 45, 46
amplification, 5, 9, 12, 18, 29, 37, 68
Article 5, 36, 65, 67
Audience Resilience, 5, 49
Authenticity, 57, 76, 77
Authoritarian, 11
Bannon, 1
Battle of Britain, 25, 26, 65
Belarus, 5, 55, 56
Birla Carbon, 3
Bots, 8
Butina, 50
CISA), 31
collective defense, 35, 36, 37, 67, 73
Collective Defense, 5, 35, 65, 72
Columbia Chemical, 3
Comet Ping Pong, 12
CrowdTangle, 9, 65, 76
Cyber, 66
debunking, 8, 9, 18, 33
deepfakes, 8, 11, 8, 32
digital, 11, 12, 50, 55, 65, 66, 68, 71, 75, 76, 77
disinformation, 7, 8, 9, 11, 4, 5, 7, 8, 9, 12, 15, 16, 17, 18, 31, 32, 36, 37, 42, 45, 46, 47, 50, 55, 57, 60, 61, 65, 66, 67, 71, 73, 74, 75, 77
Donald Mihalek, 7
Drotschmann, 15
Duterte, 1
EEAS, 55, 59
Elections, 55
emotional triggers, 4, 13, 62, 63
engagement, 11, 26, 27, 45, 47, 61, 65, 67

erosion, 49, 61
Exercises, 5, 9, 13, 20, 28, 33, 37, 44, 47, 51, 57, 62
Exhaustion, 13, 66
Fact-Checking, 66, 75
Fazze, 15
Finland, 31, 42
Firehose of Falsehood, 66
Flood, 5, 11, 13, 1, 7, 8, 11, 53, 56, 57, 66
Flood the Zone, 5, 1, 66
Global Disinformation Index (GDI, 76
Goebbels, 1
Google's Jigsaw, 31
Graphika, 5, 75
Hayden, 3, 49, 50
Hillary Clinton, 2, 11
Hitler, 1, 26
hoax, 3, 5
Humor Over Rumor, 32
Hybrid, 18, 66
Illicit SIM farms, 7
Influencers, 8
information, 7, 8, 11, 2, 3, 4, 12, 13, 15, 16, 25, 26, 27, 28, 32, 41, 49, 55, 60, 62, 63, 65, 66, 67, 74, 75, 76, 77
information discipline, 25, 65
Internet Research Agency, 1, 4
ISIS, 3
journalism, 1, 2, 73, *See*
Journalism, 5, 35
Kremlin, 32, 75
Lockdown Mode, 66, 73
Luftwaffe, 25
malinformation, 71
Mapping Motives, 6
Marat Mindiyarov, 3, 1

media literacy, 11, 31, 51, 75, 77
misinformation, 7, 13, 15, 16, 17, 21, 29, 32, 42, 46, 71, 75, 76
narratives, 5, 8, 9, 27, 32, 34, 50, 68, 71
NATO, 5, 8, 35, 36, 65, 67, 76
NATO4NEWS, 36
New Zealand, 41
Normalization, 8, 67
OSINT, 67, 76
pandemic disconformation, 15, 32, 41
pandemic disinformation, 17
Pentagon, 7, 35
Pizza-Gate, 11, 12
platforms, 3, 4, 19, 45, 46, 47, 65, 73
Pre-bunking, 5, 31, 32, 33, 67
propaganda, 2, 4, 8, 16, 31, 32, 45, 55, 66, 67, 73
provenance, 47, 57, 58, 71, 76
Putin, 2
radical transparency, 51, 72
reality, 3, 11, 12, 2, 49, 55, 56, 57, 59, 60, 66
repetition, 19, 43, 65, 66
replacement, 55
Russia, 7, 1, 4, 5, 16, 31
Savushkina, 1

scapegoating, 31
Schindler, 3, 45
SIM Farm, 67
Stalin, 1
Strategic silence, 28
Synthetic Media, 68
Takeaways, 5, 9, 13, 18, 27, 33, 36, 43, 46, 51, 57, 61, 68
telecom, 7
Troll Farm, 68
truth, 7, 8, 9, 11, 12, 1, 4, 5, 7, 12, 16, 19, 26, 37, 41, 42, 43, 44, 45, 46, 47, 49, 50, 51, 57, 59, 60, 61, 66, 67, 71, 74
Ukraine, 7, 8, 31
United Nations, 7, 36
vaccine, 16, 42
Velocity, 5
verification, 11, 28, 33, 37, 50, 51, 67, 68, 73, 75, 76
virality, 51
Visual Inoculation, 31
Wayback Machine, 9, 68, 76
Welch, 12
World Health Organization, 32
WTOP, 3, 45

NOTES

www.ingramcontent.com/pod-product-compliance
Lightning Source LLC
Chambersburg PA
CBHW052130030426
42337CB00028B/5104